WORLD BOOK
looks at

THE SEA
AND ITS MARVELS

World Book, Inc.
a Scott Fetzer Company

Chicago London Sydney Toronto

WORLD BOOK
looks at
THE SEA AND ITS MARVELS

World Book looks at
Books in this series are based on information and illustrations contained in The World Book Encyclopedia.

Created and edited by Brian Williams and Brenda Williams
Designed by Tim Mayer

World Book, Inc.
525 W. Monroe
Chicago, Illinois 60661

For information on other World Book products, call 1-800-255-1750 x2238

ISBN 0-7166-1803-6 (hard cover)
ISBN 0-7166-1811-7 (soft cover)
Library of Congress Catalog Card Number 96-61142

Printed in Mexico

1 2 3 4 5 6 7 8 9 10 99 98 97 96

CONTENTS

Introducing the
Sea and its Marvels 4

The Ocean 6

Amazing Undersea World 8

The Fish in the Sea 10

Living in Water 12

Hunters and Hunted 16

Strange Sea Shapes 20

Ocean Wanderers 22

Seashore and Sea Floor 24

Crusty Crustaceans 26

Shells of the Sea 28

Octopus and Squid 32

The Open Ocean 34

Sharks and Rays 38

Coral Reef 40

Exploring the Reef 42

The World's Biggest Reef 44

Sponges 46

Creatures of the Deep 48

Dolphins and Whales 50

Ocean Birds and Mammals 54

Marine Reptiles 58

Fascinating Facts 60

Glossary 62

Index 63

Introducing the Sea and its Marvels

We live on a watery planet and we have only just begun to explore its wonders. The sea that covers much of the earth's surface is a fascinating world of mystery.

The importance of the ocean

The sea – or ocean – is the great body of water that covers more than 70 per cent of the earth's surface. Seen from space, the earth reveals far more ocean than dry land. We may think of the sea as a place for swimming, boating, and having fun, but it provides us with much more than recreation. The ocean is an important source of food. It also produces energy and minerals. The ocean serves as a highway for ships carrying cargo between continents.

Above all else, the ocean helps keep the earth's climate balanced – by making it not too hot and not too cold, and by supplying moisture for rainfall. Without the ocean, where life began, no life could exist on our planet.

Puzzled by a new word?

To learn the meaning of a difficult or new word, turn to the glossary on page 62.

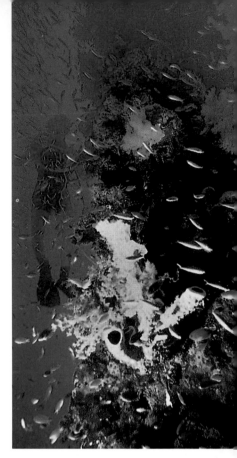

In the warm waters of the tropics, divers swim among the fishes and other sea creatures that swarm around coral reefs.

Ocean waves crash onto a rocky shore. The waters of the ocean are constantly moving in an ever-changing and dramatic spectacle.

In the polar regions, great icebergs drift in the ocean. Even in these freezing waters, life is plentiful.

The living ocean

Life on earth began in the ocean many millions of years ago. Today, an amazing variety of plants and animals live in the sea – from tiny floating plankton to enormous whales.

Some ocean animals live along the shore, where sea meets land. Many more live in the open sea, near the sunlit surface or in the darkest depths of the ocean where the water is bitterly cold.

In this book, you will meet many amazing creatures. Each is a miracle of nature, superbly adapted to life in the ocean. Yet each is only a small part of the astonishing richness of this wondrous world.

Let's take a closer look at the marvels of the living ocean.

Coral islands are found in warm oceans. An atoll forms when a ring of coral builds up on an underwater bank or on the crater of a sunken volcano. The coral forms a reef on which a layer of soil lodges and plants spring up. Atolls such as the one shown here enclose a shallow pool or lagoon.

Dolphins in the open ocean. These lively animals often swim alongside ships and occasionally come close to people swimming in the sea.

The Ocean

We depend on the ocean in many ways. By exploring the ocean to understand it, we can learn to manage its resources wisely.

How were the oceans formed?

The earth is probably at least 4.5 billion years old. Scientists think that the earth began as a mass of rock surrounded by a cloud of gas. Chemicals rising from inside the earth formed water. Over millions of years, the water slowly collected to form the oceans.

As land developed on the earth, rainwater and rivers dissolved salts and other substances from rocks and carried them to the oceans, making the waters salty. The oceans contain 97 per cent of all the water on the earth.

The three great oceans. The dark blue areas of the map show where the continents extend under the oceans, forming shallow continental shelves. The black, curving lines represent deep trenches in the ocean floor. The Mariana Trench is the deepest point in the ocean.

One great ocean

All the waters of the earth form one great world ocean. However, the continents divide the world ocean into three major parts – the Pacific Ocean, the Atlantic Ocean, and the Indian Ocean. Each ocean includes smaller bodies of water. For example, the Caribbean Sea is part of the Atlantic Ocean, and the South China Sea is part of the Pacific Ocean.

Beneath the surface

The bottom of the ocean has its own majestic seascape. Huge plains spread across the ocean floor and mountain peaks rise toward the surface. Volcanoes erupt from the ocean bottom and deep valleys cut through the floor.

A diver works on the ocean floor. People can travel underwater in small vehicles called submersibles.

DID YOU KNOW?

There is a bit of "ocean" inside us!

The body of an adult male contains almost 5 gallons (about 18 liters) of salt water. This fluid in human bodies is a lot like seawater.

Surfers ride on a wave. Many people enjoy the ocean as a place for recreation.

Constantly on the move

The vast ocean is constantly moving. Ocean currents flow through the sea just like giant rivers. Winds and earthquakes beneath the ocean create waves across the surface of the waters. The gravitational pull of the moon and sun causes movement too – the daily rise and fall of the tides.

Energy from the sea

Petroleum and natural gas are the most important mineral resources in the ocean. Offshore wells provide about 25 per cent of the world's oil. Huge deposits of oil lie undiscovered beneath the ocean.

Minerals from the sea

Seawater also contains valuable minerals, such as bromide, manganese, and salt. And the ocean floor has rich deposits of copper, iron, zinc, and other minerals.

Tidal power

Ocean tides produce energy. Tidal power stations use the energy in the rise and fall of the tides to produce electricity.

How does rain come from the sea?

Most rainfall begins in the sea. The sun's heat evaporates water from the ocean surface. The water rises as invisible vapor and forms clouds as it cools. It then falls back to earth as hail, rain, sleet, or snow.

A fishing crew hauls in a good catch. People have fished in the ocean for thousands of years. However, modern fishing boats have taken so many fish that some areas of the ocean no longer provide the rich harvests of former years.

THE BIG THREE OCEANS

The Pacific Ocean is by far the largest of the oceans.

- **It covers about 70 million square miles (181 million square kilometers) – nearly a third of the earth's surface.**

- **Next comes the Atlantic Ocean, which covers about 36 million square miles (94 million square kilometers).**

- **The Indian Ocean covers about 29 million square miles (74 million square kilometers).**

Amazing Undersea World

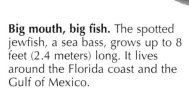

Fish are just one of the groups of animals living in the ocean. Many other kinds of animals, as well as plants, are at home there.

When did life begin in the ocean?

The earliest fossils known are about 3.5 billion years old. These fossils are primitive bacteria, including blue-green algae. Fossils of the first animals appear in rocks about 700 million years old. These early creatures were sea animals, including worms, jellyfish, and corals. Fossils of one kind of sea worm, shown in the picture below, tell us that this creature has remained unchanged for more than 500 million years!

Big mouth, big fish. The spotted jewfish, a sea bass, grows up to 8 feet (2.4 meters) long. It lives around the Florida coast and the Gulf of Mexico.

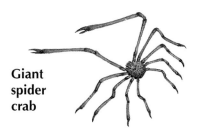

Giant spider crab

Fish in the ocean

About 13,000 species (kinds) of fish live in the ocean – almost three-fifths of all known fish. Saltwater fish are called marine fish and they can live in many kinds of ocean environments.

Many marine fish live in warm waters. More than a third of all our saltwater fish live around coral reefs in the Indian and Pacific oceans. Many kinds of fish live in temperate waters that are neither very warm nor very cold. Such waters are found north and south of the tropics. The cold waters of the Arctic and Antarctic oceans have fewer kinds of fish.

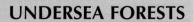

Blood-red starfish

Purple sea urchin

Flatworm

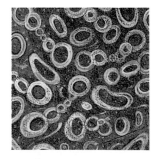

Fossils of sea worms. These animals lived in the prehistoric ocean.

UNDERSEA FORESTS

Giant kelp, a seaweed, may grow up to 200 feet (60 meters) long. Kelp forms great underwater forests in the ocean.

Fingered limpet

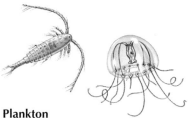

Plankton animals include copepods, which are crustaceans (animals with jointed legs and shells), and the hydromedusa, a kind of jellyfish.

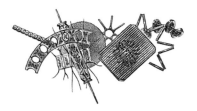

Diatoms are a type of plantlike plankton found mainly in cold waters. Some diatoms live inside tiny sea lice!

Common octopus

Other animals in the ocean

Marine animals include reptiles, mammals, mollusks, worms, and many other species. All ocean life can be divided into three groups: plankton, nekton, and benthos.

Plankton are small living things that drift with the ocean current. There are two kinds. Plantlike plankton are called phytoplankton. Plankton animals are known as zooplankton. They are so tiny that you need a microscope to see most of them.

Nekton animals can swim freely. Most live near the ocean's surface, where food is plentiful; others prefer the deep ocean.

Benthos organisms live on or near the sea floor. Where sunlight can reach the sea floor, plants such as kelp become anchored to the bottom. Animals of the benthos may burrow in the ocean floor, attach themselves to the bottom, or crawl or swim in the deepest waters.

SETTLING DOWN

Most bottom-dwelling creatures begin their lives floating with the plankton and drifting with the currents. Then they sink to the sea floor where, as adults, they become part of the benthos. Barnacles, clams, and oysters all begin as free-floaters before settling down as stay-put residents of the ocean floor.

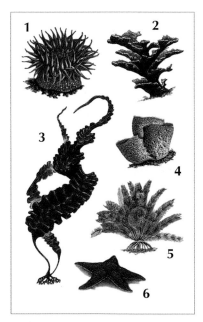

Animals that swim freely in the ocean include: reptiles (such as turtles 1), mollusks (squid 2), and mammals (sea lion 3), as well as fish 4, 5. Most free-swimmers live near the ocean's surface.

Bottom-dwellers in the ocean include: anemones 1, corals 2, seaweeds 3, sponges 4, crinoids 5, and starfish 6. Some live out their adult lives attached to the bottom in one position.

The Fish in the Sea

The first fish appeared on the earth about 500 million years ago. Some kinds of fish living today have changed little in all that time.

Jaws or no jaws

Fish are vertebrates – animals with backbones. Scientists divide fish into two main groups: fish with jaws (almost all fish) and fish without jaws (just two kinds – lampreys and hagfish).

Bones or no bones

Scientists further divide jawed fish according to the kind of skeleton they have. One group has a skeleton made of a tough, elastic substance called cartilage. This group of about 790 species includes sharks, rays, and chimaeras. Almost all of them live in salt water.

The other group has a skeleton made largely or partly of bone. These so-called bony fish make up by far the largest group – about 95 per cent of all known kinds of fish.

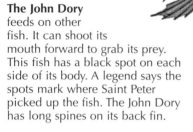

The John Dory feeds on other fish. It can shoot its mouth forward to grab its prey. This fish has a black spot on each side of its body. A legend says the spots mark where Saint Peter picked up the fish. The John Dory has long spines on its back fin.

Shark

Chimaera

Ray

The moray eel lurks in rocky crevices and around shipwrecks.

Sharks and rays are relatives, though their body shapes are different. Chimaeras, or ratfish, are also related to sharks and live near the ocean bottom.

Hagfish

Lamprey

Lampreys and hagfish are the most primitive of all fish. They have slimy bodies without scales, and no jaws.

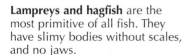

BLOODSUCKERS

Certain types of lamprey attach themselves to other fish by means of a round sucking mouthpart. The lamprey then uses its toothed tongue to cut into its victim and feed on its blood. Hagfish have slitlike mouths but no sucking organ. They eat the insides of dead fish.

LIVING FOSSIL

The coelacanth is a primitive fish that swam in the ocean more than 300 million years ago.

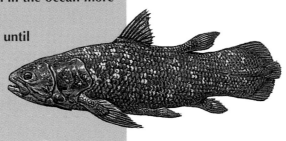

- Coelacanths were believed to be extinct until 1938, when a living coelacanth was caught off the coast of South Africa. Other coelacanths have been caught since then.

- The coelacanth uses its fins as props when it rests on the sea bottom.

- Female coelacanths give birth to live young. Most other fish lay eggs.

All kinds of fish

Today, the various kinds of fish differ from one another in so many ways that they seem to have little in common. Some are excellent swimmers, using their flexible fins to help them swim at high speed or dart in and out of coral. Other fish hardly swim at all. They lie on the ocean floor or burrow into mud.

Fish have developed a variety of shapes. Fast swimmers, such as sharks and barracuda, are streamlined for speed. Many bottom-dwellers, like flatfish and rays, are flattened from top to bottom. Some fish are long and slender, like eels. Others are chunky, like the John Dory.

The sole is hard to see until it moves. It has a flat body with both eyes on one side of its head. Like other flatfish, it lies flat on one side on the sea floor, facing up.

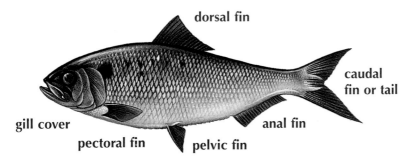

dorsal fin

caudal fin or tail

gill cover

pectoral fin

pelvic fin

anal fin

The shad is related to the herring. Like many free-swimming fish, the shad has a streamlined body, covered with tough scales and flattened from side to side. The fish uses its tail and fins to swim. Like most fish, the shad breathes through gills on each side of the head.

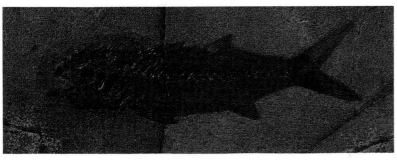

A fish that lived 58 million years ago left its "picture" in this fossil. Prehistoric fish were the first animals with backbones, and the bones of this fish can be clearly seen in the rock.

11

The **jellyfish** swims by expanding its body like an opening umbrella, then pulling it together again rapidly. This squeezes water out from beneath the body, forcing the jellyfish upward.

Living in Water

Many ocean animals cannot live out of water. Others, such as seals and turtles, can live both on land and in water. Fish are especially well adapted to living in water.

Do fish breathe?

Like all animals, fish need oxygen to change food into body energy. Fish get their oxygen from water through special organs called gills.

Most fish have four gills on each side of the head. Fish gulp water through the mouth and pump it over the gills. As the water passes over rows of fleshy, threadlike filaments in the gills, oxygen is taken from the water into the fish's bloodstream. Unwanted carbon dioxide gas is released into the water which is passed out through openings in the gills.

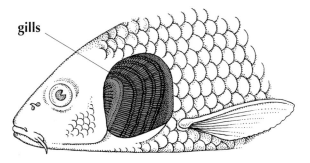

gills

Gills are the breathing organs of most fishes. The thin tissues of the gills absorb oxygen from the water.

Do fish have teeth?

Most fish have teeth and use them to seize their prey or tear off chunks of flesh. As well as having teeth rooted in their jaws, some fish have extra teeth on the roof of the mouth or on the tongue. Most fish also have teeth in the pharynx, a short tube behind the mouth. They use these teeth to crush and grind food.

Do fish sleep?

Fish have no eyelids so they cannot close their eyes to sleep. But like all animals, they need rest. Some rest on the ocean floor. Others sleep in midwater, still moving their fins. The slippery dick, a coral-reef fish, sleeps on the bottom under a covering of sand.

A lemon shark glides through the water. The three small fish riding on the shark are remoras. The remora uses a sucking disk on its head to hold onto the shark. It gets a free ride and the chance to eat scraps of the shark's food.

Mouthbreeding fish, such as this male jawfish, hold their eggs in their mouth until the eggs hatch.

Going places

Some sea animals, such as rock-clinging shellfish, stay in one place. But most marine creatures need to move around to find food.

Most fish swim by swinging their muscular tails from side to side. They use their fins to balance and steer. Dolphins and whales swim by moving their tails up and down, rather than from side to side. Turtles paddle with their flippers, as do seals. Penguins swim by using their wings as paddles.

Many tiny sea creatures, such as flatworms, swim by waving small hairlike structures – like oars. Jellyfish and squid swim by shooting out jets of water – a kind of jet propulsion.

Crabs and lobsters do not swim. Instead, they walk about on the sea floor.

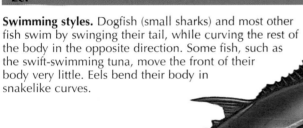

Dogfish

Tuna

Eel

Swimming styles. Dogfish (small sharks) and most other fish swim by swinging their tail, while curving the rest of the body in the opposite direction. Some fish, such as the swift-swimming tuna, move the front of their body very little. Eels bend their body in snakelike curves.

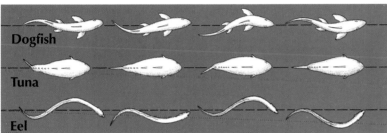

The bluefin tuna is a fast swimmer.

FISHY FACTS

● Fish cannot turn their heads, but most fish can see both right and left at the same time.

● Fish can hear sounds in the water – their ears are inside their head.

● Fish have well-developed senses of smell and taste.

● Tiny canals under the skin, known as the lateral line system, enable a fish to "feel" vibrations in the water – an early-warning "radar" of approaching danger.

The imperial angelfish lives on coral reefs. Their bright markings help angelfishes to recognize one another, but confuse predators.

Living in the ocean, fish need specialized body systems. They also have their own ways of playing hide-and-seek with enemies.

Seaweed or fish?
The sargassum fish looks so like seaweed it is almost impossible to see as it climbs about in the weeds with its pawlike fins.

Do fish drink sea water?

In the natural process called osmosis, liquid passes from a weaker solution to a more concentrated one. Ocean water is much saltier than fresh water. It is also saltier than the body fluids of the fish that live in the ocean. So marine fish constantly lose water from their body through their skin and gills into the stronger salt solution of the sea water.

To make up for this loss, ocean fish drink a lot of sea water. Their bodies get rid of the unwanted salt. Since they need almost all the water they drink, ocean fish produce only small amounts of urine.

Can river fish live in the sea?

Freshwater fish in rivers and lakes have the opposite problem. Their body fluids are saltier than fresh water, so these fish constantly take in water through their skin and gills. They get rid of the extra water in their bodies by producing a lot of urine.

The sea pen looks like a plant. But sea pens are animals without backbones, related to jellyfish and sea anemones.

Partners. A coral trout and a wrasse help each other. The small wrasse removes parasites from the gills of the coral trout. The wrasse gets a meal and the coral trout gets rid of troublesome pests.

A few fish can switch from fresh water to salt water, including salmon, eels, and sturgeon.

Safer in school

Many fish live by themselves, swimming and hunting for food alone. But in some species, large numbers of fish live together in groups called schools.

In a school, fish swim close together. Each fish then has a better chance of escaping a hungry predator than if it were swimming alone. A school often breaks up at night to feed and then regroups the next morning. However, the approach of a predator always brings the fish hurrying back to the group.

All the fish in a school are about the same size. Baby fish and adults never swim in the same school.

Safety in numbers. Thousands of sardines swim together in a school.

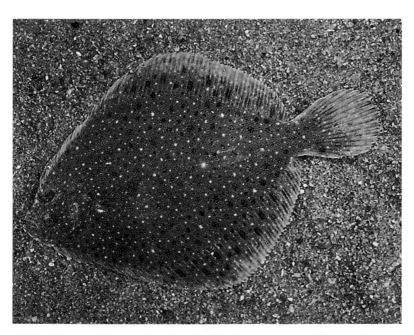

Hide-and-seek fish. The flounder can change its pattern to match the stones and sand on which it rests.

Fan worms live in tubes on the sea floor. These animals collect food from the water by waving their fanlike tentacles.

Hunters and Hunted

Some fish are plant-eaters. Others eat shellfish, worms, and other water animals. Many ocean fish eat each other. Life underwater is a constant battle between the hunters and the hunted.

Big eats small

Some fish eat mainly tiny plankton. Herring eat plankton, and so do flying fish. It's surprising to discover that the three largest fish – the whale shark, basking shark, and giant manta ray – also feed mainly on plankton.

Waste-removers

Some fish are scavengers. They eat the waste products and dead bodies of animals that sink to the bottom.

Come a little closer

Some fish use special body organs to catch food. In the dark ocean depths, certain fish attract their prey with flashing lures. Drawn to the light by curiosity, a smaller fish swims just near enough – and snap! It's a small fish dinner.

Small fish watch out if an anglerfish is nearby! This fish has a fleshy growth on its head that looks just like a tasty worm. If an inquisitive fish comes too close, the anglerfish catches a meal. The stargazer fish is another angler – its bait grows out of its mouth.

The stonefish oozes poison through spines in the fins of its back and underside. It lies half-buried in sand and mud, looking just like a stone, to ambush small fish. The fish's tail is to the left in this photograph. The artist's illustration (above) shows the stonefish more clearly.

An anglerfish has a fleshy bait growing from its head. The bait attracts small fish within reach of the anglerfish's jaws.

The stargazer's lure looks like a worm. When a small fish comes close enough, the stargazer snaps it up with amazing speed.

The sawfish uses its sawlike snout to attack other fish and dig out creatures hiding in the muddy ocean bottom.

The fins of the lionfish look like a bird's feathers, but they are as sharp as needles and give off a powerful poison.

Don't step on me! A weever fish lies almost hidden, waiting to grab passing crustaceans and worms. The poisonous spines on its back sometimes sting swimmers who tread on a weever buried in the sand. Weevers are plentiful in the Mediterranean Sea.

Chasing a meal

Some fish lurk on the sea floor or wait around corners for their next meal to swim by. But many fish and other sea creatures, such as seals and penguins, chase after their food. These animals rely on swimming faster than their prey. A few fish have specialized "weapons" – like the swordfish and the sawfish with their strange, long snouts.

Hiding and stinging

Fish that cannot outswim their predators hide among rocks or weeds. Some bury themselves in the sand on the sea floor. Some have spines that give them good protection, especially if the spines contain poison.

Some hunters also have spines. The lionfish uses its poisonous fins to attack other fish, or even human divers who swim too close. And the stonefish's deadly poison can kill a human being in minutes.

LOSE ONE, GROW ANOTHER

Crabs are protected by tough shells. But not even this armor can save a crab caught on the shore by a hungry seagull. The fiddler crab shown here has already lost its biggest claw but it may still escape with its life. If the crab can scuttle away while the gull is busy with the claw, the crab's remaining claw will enlarge and a new claw will grow in place of the lost one.

Flyingfish leap out of the water to get away from larger fish.

HOW DO FISH FLY?

- **The flyingfish launches itself out of the water with a flick of its strong tail.**

- **In the air, it glides by spreading its large fins, which act like wings.**

- **Flyingfish can fly as far as 1,000 feet (300 meters).**

- **A flyingfish can turn in midair by moving its body muscles and tail fin.**

The puffer puffs itself up like a balloon.

Fish use many unusual methods to catch food – and avoid making a meal for some other animal!

Blow-up fish

A blown-up puffer fish makes an impossible meal! The puffer can blow itself up like a balloon by filling its stomach with water or air. The puffer then swells to twice its normal size and floats on the surface. Some puffers also have prickles that stick up only when the fish is full of air.

Fast-food lookalike

Looking like another fish can be useful. The wrasse is a harmless cleaner that helpfully removes parasites from the skin of larger fish. These bigger fish welcome a wrasse swimming close to them, and seek its services. One kind of blenny looks so much like a cleaner wrasse that large fish are fooled into letting it swim close. However, instead of removing parasites, the blenny takes a fast bite out of the unlucky "customer" and makes a quick getaway!

Blenny

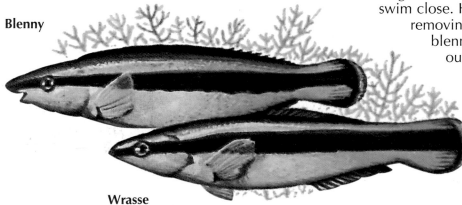

Wrasse

In disguise. By looking like a cleaner wrasse, this blenny gets a bite to eat.

The porcupinefish turns into a prickly ball when in danger. It has spines all over its body. When threatened by an enemy, the porcupinefish swallows water into its stomach to make the spines stick out.

One huge gulp

The black swallower can gulp down fish twice its size! In the deep ocean, food is scarce so this fish cannot afford to miss a possible meal. The black swallower's jaws are hinged to open very wide, and its stomach can stretch to several times its normal size. Its prey is swallowed whole and gradually digested.

A black swallower has an enormous stomach.

Fish that glow

Most fish live in the sunlit waters close to the ocean surface, but fish in the deep ocean live in darkness. Many make their own light. The lanternfish has light-making organs along the sides of its head and body. Lanternfish use their lights to communicate with one another and to attract prey.

These fish cannot be seen from below because their glowing undersides blend in with the sunlit or moonlit sea surface. From above, the lanternfish is equally hard to spot because its dark back blends in with the black water below.

The lanternfish gives off light, like more than 1,000 other species of fish.

19

Strange Sea Shapes

An animal shaped like a bottle. An animal that looks like a flower. A fish with a horse's head and a grasping tail. A creature that is not just one living thing, but hundreds! An animal that can turn itself inside out. These are just some of the ocean's marvels.

The Portuguese man-of-war

It looks like a jellyfish, but is actually a colony with hundreds of members. The colony begins with one member that grows and "buds" to produce new members. The original member then develops into a balloonlike float filled with gas. This balloon keeps the colony afloat and acts like a sail, catching the wind and moving the colony around. The animal was probably named by sailors who thought it looked like a sailing ship called a man-of-war.

Other members of this strange colony hang beneath the float. They form poisonous stinging tentacles up to 30 feet (9 meters) long that catch food for the colony. A fish that touches a tentacle is paralyzed and killed. The tentacles then haul up the food for other members to digest. Breeding members produce the eggs and sperm needed to make new colonies.

The Portuguese man-of-war floats on the surface of warm seas, tentacles dangling down into the water.

Sea squirt

Is that a leather bottle on the sea bottom? No, it's a sea squirt – an animal that spends its life attached to stones, shells, or other fixed objects. The sea squirt has two body openings. It sucks in water through one opening to get food, and squirts water out through the other.

The sea squirt never wanders from its base on the sea floor.

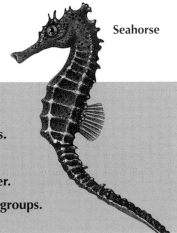

Seahorse

FATHER IN CHARGE

- The male seahorse has a pouch in which the female lays her eggs.
- He carries the eggs in the pouch for up to 45 days.
- When the young hatch, he releases tiny, live babies into the water.
- Baby seahorses often hold onto each other's tails, forming small groups.

Seahorse

This fish has a head like that of a tiny horse. The seahorse feeds by sucking small animals into its tubelike snout. It can wrap its long tail around plants and swims, weakly, by fanning its small back fin.

Flowers that sting

Sea anemones look like flowers, but they are actually animals related to jellyfish. A sea anemone clings to a rock or any undersea structure with one end of its body. At the other end, the animal has a mouth surrounded by tiny tentacles for catching food. Stinging cells in the waving tentacles throw out tiny poison threads to paralyze small sea animals. The tentacles drag the food into the anemone's mouth.

A yellow sea anemone. Sea anemones may also be blue, green, pink, red, or a colorful mixture.

A sea cucumber. In Asia, sea cucumbers are dried and sold as food called *trepang*.

Insides out

The sea cucumber is a strange animal in the starfish and sea urchin family. At one end of its soft body is the mouth, surrounded by tentacles that shoot out to grab food. On its underside, the sea cucumber has rows of tiny tube feet with suction disks on their ends, for crawling and clinging to objects.

The sea cucumber looks helpless, but it has an unusual weapon. When attacked, it throws out sticky threads from inside its body! The gooey mess distracts the enemy while the sea cucumber crawls away.

21

Ocean Wanderers

Some ocean creatures make amazing journeys during their lives. How these wanderers find their way across the ocean, often returning to the place where they were born, is a mystery of nature.

A strange life story

Eels are long, slimy fish that look like snakes. There are about 600 kinds of eels. The species known as common eels can live in both salt water and fresh water.

American and European common eels begin their lives in the Sargasso Sea, a part of the Atlantic Ocean northeast of the West Indies. They hatch from eggs into tiny transparent larvae. The larvae drift northward with the ocean currents, growing until they look like miniature eels. They are then known as elvers.

Common eels of Europe and North America leave their freshwater streams to breed in the salty Sargasso Sea. Then they die. The young eels later migrate to fresh water, as shown by the arrows on the map.

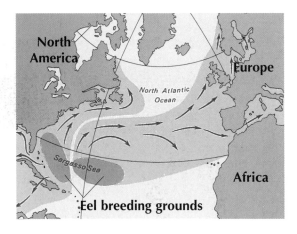

Homeward bound

Scientists believe male elvers remain in salt water, but females swim into rivers and will even climb waterfalls or dams to reach inland waters. It takes as long as 10 years for an eel to grow to adult size, when its skin is silvery and it is ready to breed. Each autumn, large numbers of silver eels group together and return to the Sargasso Sea. They swim down streams and rivers to the ocean and even wriggle overland if they find their path blocked.

How do these migrating eels find their way? Some researchers say they use their sense of smell. Others believe they rely on ocean currents for direction, sensing weak electric currents in movements of water.

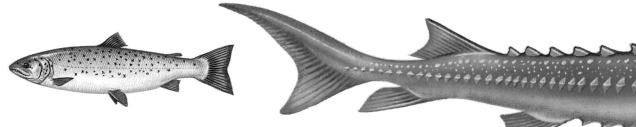

Atlantic salmon are less plentiful than Pacific salmon, and more closely related to trout. All other kinds of salmon live in the Pacific Ocean.

Sturgeon swim from the sea to lay their eggs in freshwater streams. Sturgeon eggs are used in making caviar, a tasty and expensive delicacy. The American white sturgeon shown here grows up to 20 feet (6 meters) long. The largest known Russian sturgeon, or beluga, was a giant of 28 feet (8.6 meters).

The salmon's journey

Salmon are born in fresh water but most of these fish spend part of their lives in the ocean. To reach their spawning (breeding) grounds, salmon may swim upstream for miles, battling against rushing currents and swirling rapids and leaping up waterfalls. Salmon breed in shallow, gravelly stream beds. After the female salmon lays her eggs, the male fertilizes them with sperm. Most salmon die soon after spawning.

Chinook salmon are the largest salmon.

Down to the sea

When they hatch from the eggs, baby salmon spend up to three years in freshwater streams. Sooner or later, they set off for the sea, but many young salmon die on the way. Those youngsters that reach the ocean may spend five years as saltwater fish, growing up.

Sockeye salmon, also known as blueback or red salmon, are the most valuable food salmon.

And back again

When they are ready to breed, salmon swim back to fresh water. Astonishingly, most salmon return to the stream in which they were hatched. How? In the open sea, they may navigate by sensing the magnetic field of the earth and the currents of the ocean. Near the coast, salmon apparently find their "home" stream by its scent.

Salmon leap over a waterfall as they journey upstream to spawn. The strength and determination of these powerful fish drives them on.

Most salmon make this journey once and then die. Only Atlantic salmon swim back to the sea and return to their home stream to spawn as many as three times.

Seashore and Sea Floor

Fascinating animals and plants live on the seashore and sea floor. Some are constantly battered by waves. Others are left high and dry by the daily tides. Many have shells to protect them from predators.

Seaweeds

About 7,000 kinds of seaweeds grow in the oceans. All are algae, which lack true roots, stems, leaves, and flowers. But, like land plants, algae can make their own food, using energy from sunlight.

Most seaweeds grow near coasts, clinging to rocks, shells, or the sea floor. A rootlike part, called a holdfast, anchors large seaweeds and prevents them from being washed away. Soft, flexible parts called fronds grow out from the holdfast and sway in the water. Some seaweeds have gas-filled swellings on their fronds that keep them afloat.

The **spiny lobster** lives in warm coastal waters. Unlike other lobsters, the spiny lobster has no large front claws.

Starfish come in all shapes and sizes. Most have five arms, but some starfish have 40 arms or more!

The **limpet** clings tightly to its rocky resting place.

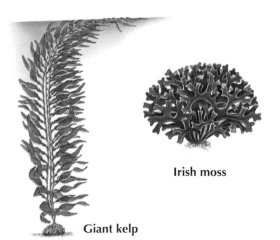

Irish moss

Giant kelp

DID YOU KNOW?

Many seaweeds are rich in vitamins and minerals. People eat seaweeds in many parts of the world.

- **Seaweed products are used in foods, drugs, cosmetics, soaps, photographic film, and paints.**

- **Irish moss, or carrageen, is used in making ice cream, toothpaste, cough syrup, and shoe polish.**

A giant clam. The shells of these huge mollusks may be up to 4 feet (1.2 meters) across.

Clinging on

If you search along a rocky seashore at low tide, you may find limpets clinging to rocks. These animals are small sea mollusks that look like saucers turned upside down. Try picking one up and you'll find that the limpet is stuck fast. The limpet's shell protects it from hungry crabs and sea birds. At high tide, the limpet lets go of the rock and crawls around, chewing on seaweeds. Before the tide goes out, the limpet latches back on to its original resting place.

Rock-chewing spine-balls

The sea urchin is a ball-shaped relative of the starfish. Its body is covered with long, movable spines that grow from a shell under the skin. The sea urchin's mouth is on the underside of its body and it scrapes up food with a set of five movable teeth. Some urchins even dig holes in rocks with their teeth! This animal has tentacles ending in suction feet and it can also push itself along with its spines.

Giant kelp plants form underwater forests. These large, branching seaweeds provide shelter for fish and other sea animals. Giant kelp is a brown alga, and prefers cold water.

SUPERSTARFISH

- **Many starfish can drop off arms to escape a predator.**
- **They can grow new arms to replace the lost ones.**
- **If a starfish is cut in two pieces, each piece may grow into a new starfish.**

A sea urchin looks like a spiny ball. A starfish is shown beside this urchin.

Most red algae are small and feathery-looking. They prefer warm seas.

Sea lettuce is a green alga. Green algae grow in both warm and cold seas.

Crusty Crustaceans

Crustaceans are animals with hard shells and many jointed legs. Crabs, lobsters, crayfish, and shrimp are crustaceans. They feed on small floating plankton, and in turn they provide food for larger animals such as fish and even some whales.

Watch out for claws

Anyone who has ever picked up a live crab or lobster knows to keep clear of the claws. The claws are front legs shaped like sharp pincers. They can give a painful nip!

Crabs and lobsters use their claws for catching food and for fighting.

Some shrimp, which look like small lobsters, have claws on their two front pairs of legs. They use their claws to dig burrows to hide in. They have other pairs of legs for walking or swimming.

An American lobster has huge front claws for grabbing and killing its prey. Lobsters eat crabs, snails, small fish – and other lobsters.

A crab starts life as an egg that hatches into a swimming larva (above). As it grows, the larva develops the legs and mouthparts of an adult crab.

A shrimp usually moves forward, but it can swim backward by flipping its fan-shaped tail.

Unlike their parents

Most crustaceans hatch from eggs as floating larvae. At first, the larva does not look at all like the adult animal. It swims weakly in the sea, gradually changing and growing until it looks like its parents.

Shedding shells

A crustacean has no skeleton inside its body, as we do. Instead, it has an exoskeleton, or external shell. However, this shell does not grow as the animal inside grows. So as a crab or lobster gets bigger, it must shed its old shell and grow a larger one.

The male fiddler crab uses its extra-large front claw to threaten and fight other males. The fiddler also waves its outsize claw around to attract females.

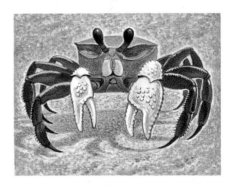

Ghost crabs live in burrows on sandy beaches. They are hard to spot if they keep still. All crabs have their eyes on stalks and walk sideways.

The hermit crab takes over the empty shell of a mollusk. When its soft body grows too big for that shell, the crab has to look for a larger one to move into.

27

Shells of the Sea

Shelled sea creatures include many kinds of mollusk, such as snails and oysters – and the barnacle, whose life story is very strange.

One shell or two?

Two large groups of ocean mollusks are the univalves (one shell) and bivalves (two shells). Limpets, snails, and whelks are univalves. These animals have one coiled shell. Some have eyes and tentacles on their heads, while others have no eyes at all. Most plant-eating univalves have thousands of weak teeth. A few kinds eat other mollusks and have several dozen strong teeth.

Shutting out danger

Bivalves include clams, oysters, and mussels. They have two shells held together by hinges that look like small teeth. Usually, the animal keeps its shells open but, when in danger, it uses strong muscles to pull the shells shut and hold them closed until the danger has passed. Bivalve mollusks have no head and no teeth. They suck in oxygen and food from the water through a muscular siphon tube.

Why oysters make pearls

Pearls are valuable gems. Oysters and some other mollusks make pearls inside their bodies, from a substance called nacre.

The oyster makes a pearl to stop itself from itching! When a bit of shell or a tiny irritating parasite gets inside the oyster, special cells in its body begin to cover the intruder with thin sheets of nacre. Layer after layer of nacre build up, forming a round pearl that has the same luster and color as the lining of the oyster's shell.

Oysters cling to rocks or other hard objects.

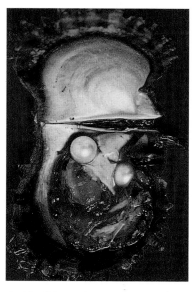

Inside this oyster are two pearls.

A BARNACLE'S LIFE

Baby barnacles have one eye, six legs, and swim about freely. As they grow, they develop two more eyes, six more legs, and two feelers. When full-grown, barnacles lose their eyes. Then they attach themselves to an object – such as a rock, a wharf, or a ship's hull. And there the barnacle stays – for the rest of its life – inside a hard, limelike box that forms around its body. To catch food, the barnacle waves its bristly legs through the open lid of the box.

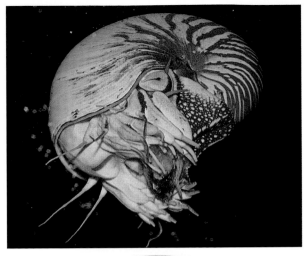

Oyster farms

In the past, most pearls were natural pearls found in oysters brought up by divers from the sea floor. Today, most pearls are cultured pearls. Cultured pearls are made by opening the shells of young oysters and placing tiny pellets of nacre or mussel shell inside. The oysters are then kept in cages. A valuable pearl is found in about 1 of every 20 of these oysters.

The chambered nautilus belongs to the squid and octopus family. The nautilus adds a larger chamber to its spiral shell each time it outgrows the old one. The big cutaway picture shows the inside of the shell (actual size).

Best foot forward

- **A sea snail has a strong, muscular foot. As the muscles of the foot move, the snail ripples along.**

- **A clam moves by pushing out its foot and hooking it in the sand. Then it pulls itself along.**

Watch out for this snail! The cone snail's poisonous sting is powerful enough to kill a person. It feeds on small sea animals.

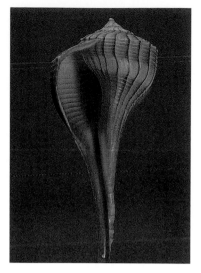

A left-handed whelk from the Atlantic coast of North America (half actual size).

Sea shells are often admired for their beautiful shape and intricate design. Many people enjoy collecting them.

Shell collecting

Shell collecting is a fascinating hobby. People also use shells to make decorations and jewelry. Shells with living animals inside them have the finest natural color and sparkle. The empty shells you pick up on the beach are usually faded by the sun and dulled by sand and seawater.

Many of the finest shells come from warm, tropical waters. In some parts of the world, sought-after shells are now rare because so many have been taken by collectors.

The shells shown on these two pages are just a few examples of the thousands of shells in the ocean.

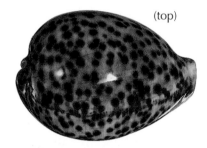

(top)

The tiger cowrie comes from the Indian and Pacific oceans (half actual size).

(underside)

Regal Murex of the Pacific coast from Mexico to Panama (half actual size).

The crown conch lives off western Florida (actual size).

The textile cone is found in the Indian and Southwest Pacific oceans (actual size).

Mantle scallop from the Pacific (actual size).

How are shells made?

Most shells have three layers. Each layer contains calcium carbonate, a kind of lime that is also found in marble and other rocks. The minerals that form the shell and give it color come from the animal's food.

Do shells grow?

Most mollusks add material to their shells throughout their lives. As long as the animal grows, the shell grows too.

Which way do shells wind?

Most snail shells wind to the right – in a clockwise direction when viewed from above. They are called right-handed shells. A few snails have left-handed shells.

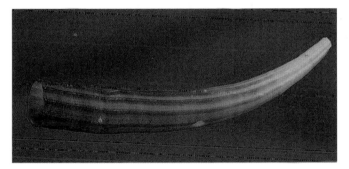

Elephant's tusk shell, a tooth shell from Japan and the Philippine Islands (actual size).

Blue mussel from the North Atlantic (half actual size).

DID YOU KNOW?

- In prehistoric times, cowrie shells and tooth shells were used as money. Native Americans in North and South America also used shells as money.

- The ancient Phoenicians and Romans made a valuable purple dye from Murex sea snails.

- In the Philippines, the thin and almost transparent shells of the Placuna oyster are used as "glass" in windows.

West Indian chiton (actual size).

31

Octopus and Squid

This baby octopus has just hatched. A female octopus has a huge family – she may lay more than 100,000 eggs! She cares for the eggs until the babies hatch. After that, the baby octopuses are on their own.

Have you ever seen a creature with eight long arms? What about an octopus – or its relative, the squid? These are interesting animals, and most are not considered dangerous to people.

Sucker arms

The octopus, squid, and the smaller cuttlefish are actually mollusks that have no outside shell. However, the octopus has long arms, or tentacles, lined with round, muscular suckers. Its arms and suckers enable the octopus to travel along the ocean floor and grab small crabs and other animals to eat.

A lot of heart

The octopus has three hearts in its soft, boneless body. Two of these hearts are associated with the gills through which the animal breathes. The eyes of an octopus are similar to human eyes, so the animal has good vision. It is also more intelligent than any other mollusk.

Not so dangerous?

The octopus has a mouth like a beak and some kinds can give a poisonous bite, but most are not dangerous to people. Stories of giant octopuses attacking divers are exciting, but the animal is not really that scary.

A giant octopus of the Pacific Ocean. The suckers along the underside of its arms produce enormous suction, giving the octopus a firm grip on rocks – or on its next meal.

The cuttlefish can pull its tentacles, or feelers, into pockets behind its eyes.

32

WOULD YOU BELIEVE?

- People once believed the argonaut sailed on water, using its long arms as sails. The animal was named for the sailors on the *Argo*, a ship whose voyage is described in the Greek myth of the Golden Fleece.

- If an octopus loses an arm, it can grow a new one.

- Octopuses do not live long. A three-year-old octopus is very old.

- Pet canaries and parrots are fed with cuttlebone – the chalky inner shell of cuttlefish.

Monsters and midgets

The largest octopus is the giant octopus of the Pacific Ocean, which can measure more than 20 feet (6 meters) across its body from arm-tip to arm-tip. The smallest octopus lives in the Indian Ocean and is only about 1 inch (2.5 centimeters) across. Squid can be much bigger – more than 40 feet (12 meters) long.

The squid has eight arms and two long tentacles with two or more rows of sucking disks used to catch prey.

Jet getaway

A squid swims like a jet flies – by propulsion. The squid draws water into folds in its body, then shoots the water out through a funnel beneath the head. This "jet" action propels the animal along. An octopus can do the same, shooting backward suddenly if a seal or whale tries to catch it.

Inky tricks

To escape danger, an octopus can also spurt dark, inky fluid into the water. Some can even produce their ink cloud in an octopus shape! Then, while the enemy tries to eat the ink cloud, the real octopus swims away. Octopuses and squid can also change color rapidly to startle a predator, or to blend in with their surroundings.

The argonaut lives in warm seas. The male, shown here, has no shell and is just half the size of a person's thumb. The female argonaut is six times bigger.

A nursery shell

An argonaut, or paper nautilus, looks like a small squid. Two of the female argonaut's arms are fan-shaped. Held together, they gradually form a stiff paperlike shell that protects the argonaut's eggs. After the eggs hatch, the argonaut casts away the nursery shell.

The Open Ocean

Some saltwater fish live along the coasts of continents. Others live far out in the open ocean, though many of these fish sometimes swim near the shore.

On the shelf

Many kinds of fish, as well as other animals, live on the continental shelf – the submerged land at the edge of the continents. Here the water is fairly shallow, sloping from the shore to an average depth of about 430 feet (130 meters).

Sunlight and darkness

In the open sea, the upper waters sparkle with sunlight. Light from the sun can reach down to about 600 feet (180 meters) and dim sunlight penetrates to about 3,000 feet (910 meters). Below that level, there is little or no light and it is very cold. Some fish – swordfish, for example – stay in the watery depths during the day and swim near the surface at night.

The manta ray is a harmless giant – up to 22 feet (7 meters) across. Despite its size, it feeds peacefully on plankton, swimming gracefully through the sunlit waters of the open ocean.

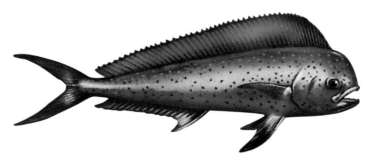

The dolphin fish lives in warm seas.

Why do swordfish have swords?

The "sword" of the swordfish is its long, flattened upper jaw, or bill. Its strong, sharp edges make an ideal weapon for defense or to stun and kill other fish for food. Swordfish have even been known to attack boats.

Swordfish

Hunters of the open sea

Hunters of the upper waters include fast swimmers like marlin and tuna. These large, powerful fish feed on smaller fish, and in turn are caught by sports fishermen and fishing fleets. The dolphin fish, also called the dorado, is another fast swimmer. It sometimes chases flyingfish.

The blue marlin has a snout like a pointed spear. Its crescent-shaped tail drives it through the water at great speed.

Millions of herring

Smaller fish such as herring swim in the open ocean too. Millions of herring swim close together near the surface and these tasty fish are caught in huge numbers by fishing boats. Herring also have many natural enemies including larger fish, dolphins, and sea birds.

A female herring may lay 185,000 eggs, which settle on the bottom, covering seaweed and rocks. Many of these eggs – and the young herring – are eaten by crabs and other fish such as haddock. Only a few of the vast number of herring eggs grow into adults.

The Atlantic herring is an important food fish. Herring swim together in large groups called shoals.

A striped marlin leaps out of the water. Marlins often leap high in the air.

Fierce hunters, floating giants – and even fish with teeth that can crack crab shells – live in the coastal waters and open ocean. Other fish provide valuable food for people.

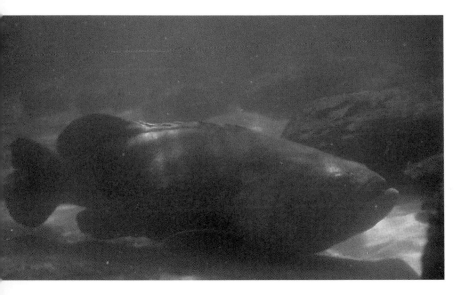

The enormous jewfish, a type of grouper, keeps close to the bottom in coastal waters. It is a slow swimmer. While barracuda and other hunters dart about in search of food, many other ocean fish move slowly - unless stirred to action by the chance of catching a bite to eat.

BARRACUDA! – Bad for You

Beware of the great barracuda – the tiger of the sea. This fierce fish not only attacks people, but it is dangerous even when it's dead. Eating its flesh – or the flesh of other tropical barracudas – frequently causes ciguatera, a disease that can kill.

The great barracuda
swims in the western Atlantic Ocean. It is the largest of the barracudas – a group of swift, fearless hunters with razor-sharp teeth. Barracudas prowl in shallow waters, but often roam far from shore as well. A great barracuda may be 6 feet (1.8 meters) long.

Wolffish are named for the large, fanglike front teeth they use to tear apart their food. Wolffish jaws can crush the shells of clams, crabs, and other hard-shelled animals. These aggressive fish attack when they are threatened.

The haddock looks like a cod, but is smaller. Also, the haddock has a black spot behind its head and a black line along each side. Haddock swim in groups along the ocean floor.

Floating giant. This strange, clumsy-looking creature is the ocean sunfish. It has no scales and no tail and looks like a huge head with pointed fins. Sunfish grow to 11 feet (3.4 meters) and weigh 1,000 pounds (450 kilograms). These giant fish often rest on the surface in sunny weather, with one fin above the water.

HOLY FISH! – And Good to Eat

Like other flatfish, the halibut is good to eat. Its name comes from the word "holy," because halibut was once a favorite dish on Christian holy days.

The Pacific halibut is a large flatfish with both eyes on the same side of its head. Its eyes lie on its right side, which is dark brown. The left side (the underside) is white. A big Pacific halibut reaches 9 feet (2.7 meters) long.

Cod is an excellent food fish. Cod live near the ocean floor in northern waters, but often swim near the surface to feed.

Sharks and Rays

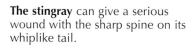

The shark, perhaps the most feared sea animal, has been swimming in the ocean for about 400 million years.

New teeth, no bones

Sharks and rays have a skeleton without bones. Instead, it is made of a tough, elastic substance called cartilage. Most sharks swallow their prey whole, or tear off large pieces of flesh with their sharp teeth. Sharks have several rows of teeth and new teeth regularly replace the old ones.

The stingray can give a serious wound with the sharp spine on its whiplike tail.

Sting in the tail

Rays and skates are related to sharks. Most rays live on the sea floor, feeding on other bottom-dwelling animals such as shellfish. Rays have flat bodies that seem to fly through the water, with graceful beats of their winglike fins.

Stingrays have poisonous spines on the tail. If a swimmer steps on a stingray, its tail swings upward and causes a painful wound that is almost as dangerous as a poisonous snakebite.

The skate uses its tail as a rudder for steering. The skate's tail also contains electric organs that help the fish find food.

SWIMMING NOSES

Sharks are superb hunters. They have excellent hearing and see well, even in dim light. Sharks have been called "swimming noses" because of their keen sense of smell. They also use a special food-finding sense to pick up tiny electrical fields given off by other fish.

The gaping jaws of a great white shark. These dangerous sharks prey on such large animals as sea lions, tuna, and other sharks. They may attack people — and even fishing boats!

How dangerous are sharks?

Sharks are not generally as dangerous as many people believe. Of about 370 kinds of sharks, only 50 species may attack human beings. Scientists do not know why these fish sometimes attack and at other times leave people alone, but most shark attacks do not result in death or serious injury.

Swimmers should take special care in areas where sharks may be found, however, and follow all safety rules. Never swim alone, at night, or in dirty water where a shark would be hard to spot. And never swim with an open wound, because blood attracts sharks. Leave the water immediately if a shark is sighted, and try to swim smoothly because thrashing movements might attract the shark's attention.

The oceanic whitetip shark has the graceful shape of many sharks. Its streamlined body glides through the water. White markings on the tips of its fins give this shark its name.

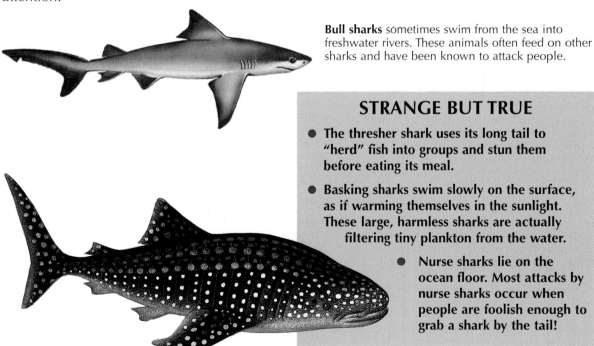

Bull sharks sometimes swim from the sea into freshwater rivers. These animals often feed on other sharks and have been known to attack people.

STRANGE BUT TRUE

- The thresher shark uses its long tail to "herd" fish into groups and stun them before eating its meal.

- Basking sharks swim slowly on the surface, as if warming themselves in the sunlight. These large, harmless sharks are actually filtering tiny plankton from the water.

- Nurse sharks lie on the ocean floor. Most attacks by nurse sharks occur when people are foolish enough to grab a shark by the tail!

The harmless whale shark is the biggest of all sharks. It can be up to 40 feet (12 meters) long, but eats only plankton and small fish.

The Coral Reef

What is coral?

Coral looks like rock and it is – a form of limestone made in the sea by millions of tiny animals. Coral grows in many fantastic shapes: branching trees, domes, crusts, and delicate pipes. The living animals that form coral also color it in beautiful shades: tan, orange, yellow, purple, and green.

How coral forms

The coral animals, called polyps, belong to the same animal group as jellyfish and sea anemones. Most are no bigger than your thumbnail, with tube-shaped bodies and tentacles. Coral polyps live together in colonies, taking in calcium from seawater to build their limestone skeletons. Then they lay down limestone (calcium carbonate) to make a solid base around the lower half of their bodies. As new polyps grow, the limestone mass grows larger and larger. When a coral polyp dies, its limestone "skeleton" remains. In this way, these animals build the great barriers and ridges called coral reefs.

Coral islands

Sometimes coral masses build up so high that they rise above the water. Waves break up coral growths and pile them up. Algae then cement the piles together to make a solid structure and, over time, soil lodges on the coral. Seeds from land plants blown by the wind or washed ashore can then take root. Many islands in the Pacific Ocean were made this way.

Sea fan corals

Reef-building corals

Mushroom corals

Coral reefs look like lovely undersea gardens. Many sea animals live among the corals, including fish, starfish, and sea anemones.

CORAL NEEDS SUNSHINE

Reef corals cannot live without special algae (simple organisms that live in water). The algae live on the polyps and the polyps use food made by the algae. The algae also help the polyps build their limestone skeletons. Like plants, algae need sunlight to live, so coral reefs grow only in sunlit water.

Exploring the Reef

Moorish idol

Clown anemone fish

A fierce reef hunter. The speckled moray eel lurks in and around coral reefs. It catches smaller fish to eat, attacking with lightning speed.

Imagine you are a diver exploring a coral reef. Swimming among the corals, you'll see many strange and colorful fish.

Fish of coral reefs

The clear, sunlit waters of a reef swarm with fish that dart in and out of the coral. Some, such as parrotfish and surgeonfish, eat algae and grasses. Others, including triggerfish and trunkfish, eat small water animals as well. Still others are hunters that catch smaller fish. Hunters of the reef include the fierce moray eel and the grouper with its large, gaping mouth.

Longspine squirrelfish

Trumpetfish

Blue tang surgeonfish

Blue trunkfish

Divers in scuba gear can explore the reef's wonders, swimming with the fishes.

DID YOU KNOW?

● Breath-holding divers searched for shells in the Mediterranean Sea as long ago as 4500 B.C.

● Divers in the Persian Gulf used goggles made of polished clear tortoise shell as early as A.D. 1300.

● The first safe and simple breathing device for free divers was the aqualung, invented in 1943.

Diving underwater

Divers who swim without breathing aids can hold their breath for little more than a minute. Some skilled free divers can swim down to 100 feet (30 meters) and stay underwater for as long as two minutes.

Scuba-diving gear allows divers to stay underwater much longer. The word scuba stands for self-contained underwater breathing apparatus. A scuba diver wears metal tanks that hold compressed air or a mixture of breathing gases. The diver breathes air from the tanks through a hose. Scuba divers also wear a face mask, and fins on their feet to help them swim.

Long-nosed butterflyfish

Nassau grouper

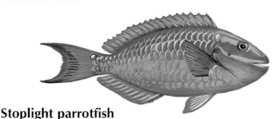

Stoplight parrotfish

Clown triggerfish

The World's Biggest Reef

Attack of the reef-eaters

The crown-of-thorns starfish eats the living parts of corals. First, the starfish wraps its arms around the coral. Then its stomach comes out of its mouth to digest the soft parts of the coral, leaving the skeleton behind. From time to time, large numbers of these starfish suddenly appear, feed in large groups, and then disappear. These crown-of-thorns starfish kill almost all the corals on a reef. Scientists are trying to find out what sets off these mass attacks.

The Great Barrier Reef lies off the northeast coast of Australia. It is the largest coral reef on earth, one of the natural wonders of the world.

The Great Barrier Reef stretches for about 1,250 miles (2,010 kilometers). It is made from about 400 different kinds of corals and is now the world's biggest marine park, protected by the Australian government. Tourists view its wonders from underwater observatories and from glass-bottomed boats.

Life on the reef

About 1,500 kinds of fish live around the reef, which also attracts many sea birds, crabs, clams, sea urchins, starfish, sea cucumbers, sponges, sea anemones, worms, and sea turtles.

The Great Barrier Reef is a huge series of coral formations, including thousands of small islands and many individual reefs.

How old is the reef?

Experts put the age of the Great Barrier Reef at between 18 and 30 million years, but much of the reef we see today is much younger. The topmost layers of reef at sea level are only a few thousand years old. However, most of these "young" reefs are built upon older reefs.

Lively and colorful fish create almost constant movement among the coral. A reef like the one shown here may contain 3,000 different species of sea animals.

Sponges

Many sponges look like plants, but these undersea curiosities are actually animals.

Some sponges are round, while others are vase-shaped. Many simply develop the shape of the object on which they grow, forming a living crust. They range in color from bright yellow, orange, or purple, to gray or brown.

Purple vase sponge

What do sponges eat?

Sponges suck in their food from the sea. The sponge takes in water through small openings in its body, and feeds on the tiny plants and animals in the water. Waste products and water leave the sponge's body through a larger opening.

Purple tube sponge

Sponges in the bath

- For centuries, people have used sponges for cleaning and bathing.

- The skeletons of certain sponges make good cleaning tools because they are soft and absorb large amounts of water.

Red-beard sponge

46

Bath sponges

Most sponges have a skeleton made of either limestone (calcium carbonate) or silica, a glasslike substance. In bath sponges, the skeleton is made of protein fibers that stay soft when the animal dies. For hundreds of years, people have used these sponges for cleaning and bathing, because they are soft and soak up a lot of water.

Today, the sponge In your bath is more likely to be an artificial one. But bath sponges are still harvested in the Gulf Stream and the Mediterranean Sea.

Yellow tube sponge

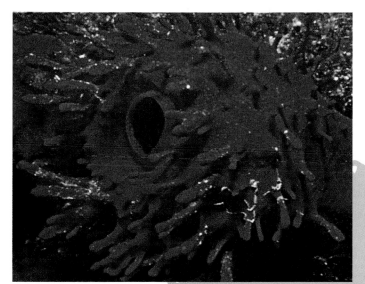

Can you guess the name of this sponge?

- **Moon sponge?**
- **Cheese sponge?**
- **Golf ball sponge?**

INDESTRUCTIBLE!

- Sponges are among the oldest kinds of animals. There were sponges in the prehistoric oceans, more than 500 million years ago.

- Some sponges live as deep as 23,000 feet (7,000 meters) in the ocean.

- Sponges can grow back together after their bodies are broken up! If a sponge is pressed through very fine cloth, it breaks into clumps of tiny cells. Put back in water, the cells first cluster together, then form complete sponges again.

ANSWER

Golf ball sponge

Creatures of the Deep

Deep-sea fish live in a dark, cold world. We know little about such fish because most kinds seldom, if ever, come to the surface.

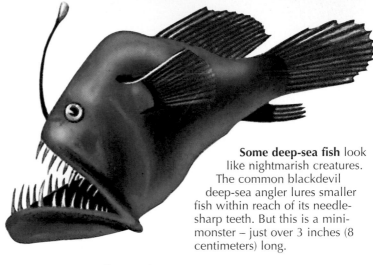

Some deep-sea fish look like nightmarish creatures. The common blackdevil deep-sea angler lures smaller fish within reach of its needle-sharp teeth. But this is a mini-monster – just over 3 inches (8 centimeters) long.

Deep-sea fish

Many deep-sea fish have large eyes, huge mouths, and sharp teeth. They look monstrous, but most are very small. Food is hard to find in their dark, deep-sea world. Some have body-lights that flash on and off in the darkness to attract prey.

The sea lily may look like a flower; but it's really a deep-sea animal.

Hot spots

On the sea floor, as deep as 10,000 feet (3,000 meters), vents like fountains gush out hot water that is rich in minerals such as copper, iron, and zinc. These vents are like oases in a deep-sea desert and communities of animals live around them. Bacteria living on chemicals in the hot water are eaten by larger creatures such as fish, crabs, shrimp, clams, and giant red tubeworms up to 12 feet (3.7 meters) long.

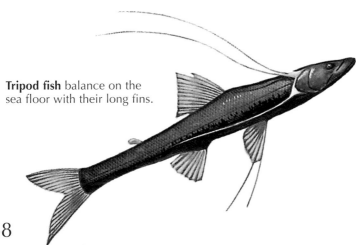

Tripod fish balance on the sea floor with their long fins.

Scientists explore the ocean depths in submersibles like the U.S. *Alvin.* This craft carries people to the ocean floor to gather samples and take photographs from inside with the aid of powerful lights.

Exploring the depths

To explore the ocean depths, scientists use small submarines called submersibles. Some submersibles carry people, and scientists take photographs from inside the craft with the aid of powerful lights. They also use a mechanical arm to gather samples from the ocean. Other submersibles carry television cameras instead of people and are guided by remote control from a ship on the surface.

The umbrella mouth gulper eel gulps down anything it can swallow.

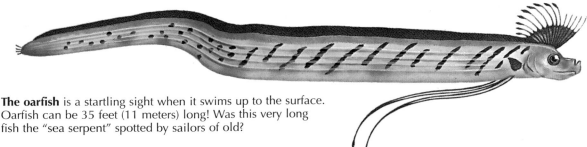

The oarfish is a startling sight when it swims up to the surface. Oarfish can be 35 feet (11 meters) long! Was this very long fish the "sea serpent" spotted by sailors of old?

Dolphins and Whales

Bottle-nosed dolphins seem to enjoy human company. You may see these dolphins in zoos and aquariums.

Dolphins and their close relatives, porpoises, are mammals. So are the biggest of all the animals that live in the ocean – the whales.

Superswimmers

The bodies of the dolphin and the porpoise are adapted for fast swimming. Their paddle-shaped front limbs, or flippers, are ideal for making sharp turns and sudden stops. The powerful tail moves up and down to drive the animal through the water.

Baby dolphins are born in the water. Then the mother and other female dolphins push the baby to the surface for its first breath of air.

Killer whales are the largest dolphins. They hunt seals and small dolphins, and will also attack larger whales. Killer whales are not known to harm people.

Hi there! A killer whale shows its teeth. Like all dolphins, killer whales use their teeth to catch prey but not to chew it. They swallow their food whole.

Coming up for air

Like all mammals, dolphins have lungs and must come to the surface regularly to breathe air. Dolphins, and whales too, breathe through an opening called a blowhole on top of the head. The blowhole is sealed shut when the dolphin is underwater.

Echo-finding

Dolphins can hear sounds too low, and too high, for human ears. They use sound to find their way and to locate objects underwater. The dolphin makes clicking noises that ripple away from its head. Echoes are produced when the sounds reflect from an object. The echoes tell the dolphin where the object is.

Common dolphins often swim in large groups. These playful animals sometimes follow ships for miles, leaping out of the water and turning somersaults.

DID YOU KNOW?

How long do dolphins live?

About 25 years. Sharks are the dolphin's main natural enemy.

Why do sailors think dolphins bring good luck?

The ancient Greeks considered dolphins to be sacred animals. For centuries, sailors have believed that dolphins swimming near their ship bring a smooth voyage.

Can dolphins talk to each other?

Dolphins "talk" using a series of whistles and clicks. They also slap their tails on the surface of the water to communicate.

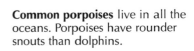

Common porpoises live in all the oceans. Porpoises have rounder snouts than dolphins.

Most whales are enormous. The blue whale is the biggest animal that has ever lived.

From land to sea

The ancestors of whales lived on land and had four legs. Then, over millions of years in the sea, the front legs developed into flippers. The back legs disappeared. Two tiny bones hidden in the hip muscles are all that remain of the whale's back legs.

The blue whale grows up to 100 feet (30 meters) and weighs more than 150 short tons (135 metric tons). In the past, it was overhunted by people for its blubber, for food, and for whale oil. This gentle giant is now rare.

With teeth and without

The baleen whales have no teeth. They strain food from the water through hundreds of thin plates in their mouths. Large baleen whales, such as the blue whale, feed mainly on the tiny sea animals that form floating plankton.

Toothed whales, like the sperm whale, have teeth and eat larger food, such as squid. There are 10 kinds of baleen, or toothless, whales and about 65 kinds of toothed whales.

SINGING WHALES

- **Whales make a variety of sounds, and they can also tell where an underwater sound is coming from.**

- **Whale calls travel far. The deep moans of a blue whale can be heard more than 50 miles (80 kilometers) away.**

- **Humpback whale songs last up to 20 minutes. All the male humpbacks in one area sing basically the same song. Humpbacks in other areas sing different songs.**

A right whale leaps from the water. Despite their size, whales are remarkable athletes.

Keeping close

Whales live in groups called herds, pods, or schools. Being together is important for many of these animals, especially for toothed whales. A mother whale stays close to her baby for at least a year. Other females may help a mother when her baby is being born in the water. Mothers and daughters sometimes stay together for life.

DEEP BREATHERS

Most whales come up to the surface for air every 5 to 15 minutes. But a sperm whale can hold its breath for two hours!

A mother humpback whale gives her baby a ride. The baby rests on its mother's back as she swims along just beneath the surface of the water.

WHAT ABOUT WHALES?

Whales have smooth, rubbery skin and hardly any hair apart from a few bristles on the head.

A layer of fat beneath the skin keeps whales warm. This fat is called blubber.

A baby whale is already a giant. Newborn blue whales are about 23 feet (7 meters) long.

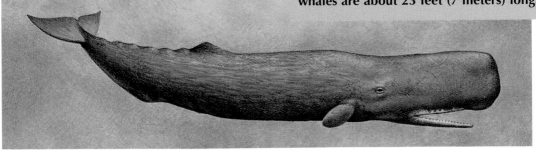

The sperm whale is the biggest toothed whale, growing up to 60 feet (18 meters) long. Sperm whales dive deep into the ocean to catch large squid.

Ocean Birds and Mammals

The gannet makes a nest of seaweed on rocky cliffs. It catches fish by diving into the water.

Animals of many kinds are found everywhere in the ocean. Some of the birds that find their food in the sea hardly ever come to land.

The wandering albatross

The wandering albatross is a large bird of the southern seas. It visits land only to breed, nesting on remote islands. The rest of its life it spends at sea. Sometimes it follows ships for days, gliding through the air with hardly a beat of its very long wings.

Gulls

Most sea birds can fly. The gulls that are so familiar around seacoasts and ports seem to glide effortlessly on outstretched wings. Like many sea birds, gulls have webbed feet, and often swim or rest on the water. At sea, flocks of gulls follow ships, waiting to pick up food scraps thrown overboard. They fly inland, too, to feed on farms and around cities.

Petrels seldom come to land, except to breed or when blown ashore by storms. Storm petrels, like the Wilson's storm petrel shown here, glide just above the waves, paddling their feet in the ocean. They seem to be walking on the water as they pick up food from the surface.

Ring-billed gull

Herring gull

Great black-backed gull

Gulls live along coasts and inland waters.

Puffins nest on cliffs beside the sea. They live in Arctic waters and swim and dive to catch small fish.

Penguins are excellent swimmers. Adélie penguins travel in a series of leaps and dives along the surface.

Penguins

Penguins live in the southern half of the world. These unusual birds stand upright and cannot fly. On land, a penguin walks with a clumsy waddle that makes people laugh. But in the water, this bird is a graceful swimmer. It has webbed feet and stubby wings that serve as paddles. The penguin's short, dense feathers form a waterproof coat, while a thick layer of body fat keeps the bird warm in cold water.

Round-the-world champion flier

Terns are sea birds famous for their flying feats of speed and distance. The Arctic tern is often called the migration champion of the world, because it migrates over a greater distance than any other bird. Some Arctic terns travel 22,000 miles (35,400 kilometers) in a year, from the Arctic Circle to the Antarctic Circle – and back again.

Arctic tern

A male Adélie penguin holds an egg between his feet. These penguins live in the Antarctic and the male bird protects the egg to keep it warm. He will not eat until the chick inside the egg has hatched – from 33 to 38 days!

Sea otters, seals, and walruses are among the mammals of the ocean.

Seals

Seals are excellent swimmers, but – unlike whales and dolphins - they can also move about on land. The seal's front feet are shaped like large paddles, for swimming, and its short back feet also serve as flippers.

Fighting for mates

Seals come ashore to give birth to their young. As many as 150,000 seals may gather at one breeding ground, called a rookery. Males fight for the best spots and collect as many females as they can. The biggest and toughest males may have as many as 100 mates!

Galapagos sea lions live on the Galapagos Islands, off the coast of Ecuador.

Fur seals start life in a group with many other pups and their mothers. Each mother returns from hunting at sea to feed her own baby.

A sea otter swims mostly on its back, paddling with its back feet while it holds stones and shellfish in its front paws. Sea otters, unlike other otters, are rarely seen on land. They eat and sleep in the sea, often resting on masses of floating seaweed. Sea otters live in the North Pacific Ocean.

Fast flippers

Fur seals, sea lions, and walruses walk on all four flippers. On land, they move faster than the seals that wriggle along by rippling their strong belly muscles. But even some of these seals can move fast! On land or ice, for example, a crabeater seal can squirm along almost as fast as a person can run.

TOOLS AND WEAPONS

- A walrus defends itself from polar bears with its ivory tusks, which are actually extra-long teeth. It also uses the tusks as hooks to climb onto ice floes.

- To open a clam for dinner, the sea otter balances a stone on its belly and bangs the shellfish on the stone.

The walrus spends much of its time in the water, looking for clams to eat. Walruses are the only seals with tusks.

Marine Reptiles

The green turtle, hunted for food in many parts of the world, is now rare.

Did you know there were seaweed-eating lizards in the ocean, as well as turtles, snakes, crocodiles, and sea cows?

Babies in danger

Sea turtles swim by beating their flippers – much as a bird flaps its wings. Unlike land turtles, they cannot pull back into their shells when danger threatens and so they rely on fast swimming to escape from predators.

Female turtles swim long distances to the beaches where they lay their eggs. When they reach land, they drag themselves out of the sea and onto the sand, bury their eggs, and then return to the water. When the baby turtles hatch, they dig themselves out of their sand holes and scramble toward the water as fast as they can. This is a danger-filled dash. So many animals prey on turtle eggs and newborn turtles that only a few babies make it safely to the ocean.

The saltwater crocodile is one of the largest crocodiles. This fierce reptile is found far out to sea from India to northern Australia, and in parts of the Pacific Ocean.

Marine iguanas live on the rocky shores of the Galapagos Islands. These are the only lizards known to feed in the ocean. They dive into the sea and swim out into the surf to eat seaweed. After their swim, they like to sunbathe on the rocks to warm up.

Sea snakes live in the warm waters of the Indian and Pacific oceans, swimming with wavelike movements of their bodies. This is an olive sea snake.

The yellow-bellied sea snake is flattened sideways, its tail forming a paddle.

Sea snakes

All snakes can swim, but sea snakes have a body shape that makes them especially good swimmers. Sea snakes prefer warm coastal waters. From time to time, huge groups of these animals are spotted in the open sea – possibly massed together by ocean currents. But stay away from sea snakes. They have a poisonous bite.

The dugong lives in the Red Sea and the Indian Ocean, eating plants that grow in the water.

Sea cows

Look at this picture of a dugong. It's hard to believe that sailors of old thought these animals were mermaids! No one could call a dugong pretty, but these rare and harmless animals have a charm all their own. Dugongs and their relatives, the manatees, are sometimes called "sea cows" because they graze on water plants.

Dolphin

Fascinating Facts

Biggest waves

The biggest waves in the world are *tsunamis*, caused by earthquakes on the sea floor or by hurricanes. On the surface of the open ocean, *tsunamis* can barely be seen, but they travel as fast as a jet airliner. As they near a coast, they slow down and may pile up in a wall of water more than 100 feet (30 meters) high.

Deepest ocean

The Pacific has an average depth of 12,900 feet (3,900 meters). Its deepest known spot is the Challenger Deep in the Mariana Trench of the western Pacific Ocean, near the island of Guam. The Challenger Deep, the deepest hole on earth, lies 36,198 feet (11,033 meters) below sea level.

Brightest swimmer

Dolphins rank top of the class among sea animals. Many scientists believe that dolphins are the most intelligent of animals, along with chimpanzees and dogs.

Sailfish

Fastest swimmer

The sailfish is said to be the fastest saltwater fish, with a top speed of 65 mph (105 kph).

Biggest crustacean

The giant spider crab measures more than 11 feet (3.5 meters) between outstretched claws.

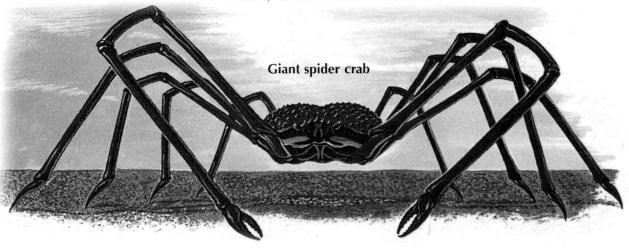

Giant spider crab

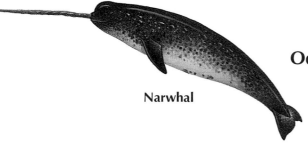

Narwhal

Oddest-looking?

The male narwhal, a small whale of the Arctic, has a long spiral tusk growing out of its upper jaw. The tusk is really the narwhal's only tooth, but what the animal does with it is not clear. It may stir up sand to find food, or use the tusk in play fights with other narwhals.

Biggest mollusk

The giant squid is a monster that measures up to 60 feet (18 meters) long – including its two long tentacles.

Most numerous fish

The bristlemouth, a tiny saltwater fish, is the most plentiful fish in the sea. Scientists believe that bristlemouths number in the billions of billions.

Biggest seal

This is the elephant seal, so called because its large nose looks a bit like an elephant's trunk. A big male southern elephant seal may be 21 feet (6.4 meters) long and weigh up to 8,000 pounds (3,600 kilograms).

Elephant seal

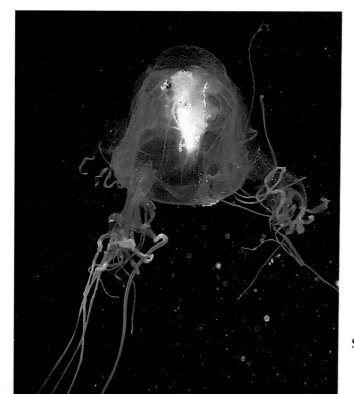

Quick killer

The sea wasp, a dangerous jellyfish, lives in the waters of the Great Barrier Reef off the coast of Australia. A severe sting from a sea wasp can kill a person in three minutes.

The largest fish

The whale shark dwarfs the largest land animal. This harmless shark may weigh twice as much as an African elephant.

Whale shark

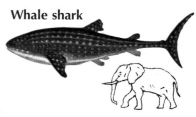

Sea wasp

61

Glossary

alga (plural: **algae**) Simple type of water organism. Seaweeds are algae.

calcium carbonate A white mineral found in limestone, marble, and coral.

cell The tiny unit of living matter that makes up all animals and plants.

climate the usual weather of a place.

colony A group of animals of the same kind living together.

continent One of the major landmasses of the earth.

continental shelf Area of shallow water around the edge of the continents.

earthquake A sudden shaking of the ground, caused by movements of rocks below the surface of the earth.

exoskeleton A skeleton that is outside the body, as in crabs and lobsters.

fertilization In reproduction, when male and female eggs combine to form a new living thing.

flipper A wide, flat limb of certain animals, used for swimming. Seals, whales, penguins, dolphins, and turtles have flippers.

fossil The remains of an animal from the distant past, preserved by becoming hard as rock.

gravity The force that keeps the planets in orbit, makes things fall to the ground when dropped, and causes the ocean tides.

hatching When a baby animal such as a fish or bird emerges from its egg.

holy Sacred. A holy day is a religious holiday.

larva The early stage of life in some animals, when they may look quite unlike their parents.

lure A bait, something that attracts a hungry animal.

marine Describes anything to do with the sea.

migration Leaving one place to settle in another. Some animals *migrate*.

myth An old story that tries to explain something in nature or something that happened long ago.

nacre Smooth, shiny substance also called mother-of-pearl.

navigate To find the way, often used of ships at sea.

organ Specialized part of the body that does a particular job, such as the heart or eye.

osmosis The movement of liquid from one solution to another through a membrane, such as skin.

paralyze To cause loss of movement. Some animals paralyze prey by using poison.

parasite A plant or animal that lives on another plant or animal, and takes food from it.

planet A heavenly body that travels around a star.

plankton Tiny animals and algae that float near the surface of the ocean.

polyp Tiny coral animal, cylinder-shaped with a mouth surrounded by tentacles.

predator An animal that feeds on other animals.

prehistoric Belonging to a time before the recording of history began.

prey An animal that is hunted by another animal for food.

remote control Operating a machine from a distance, without touching it.

sample A part of something that shows what the rest is like. Scientists collect samples – or small amounts – of seawater, rock, and living things when studying the ocean.

scale Tough, protective covering of most jawed fish. Scales overlap one another.

sea serpent Legendary sea animal described in sailors' stories.

shellfish Name given to water animals with hard outer coverings, such as clams and crabs.

solution A liquid that contains a solid or a gas dissolved in it.

spawning Breeding; in fish the laying and fertilizing of eggs.

species A group of living things with similar characteristics. Animals of the same species can breed with one another.

streamlined Having a smooth shape that enables an object or an animal to move more quickly through air or water.

submersible Undersea craft like a small submarine.

tentacle Long, thin, flexible arm of certain animals, used for feeling, grasping, or moving.

tropics The area of the earth lying just to the north and south of the equator.

tusk An extra-long tooth that extends from the jaw in some animals.

urine Fluid waste produced by the body.

vent An opening, in the sea floor or in an animal's body.

volcano An opening in the earth's surface through which melted rock, ash, and hot gases are forced out.

voyage A journey in a ship across the ocean.

Index A page number in **bold** type indicates a picture

albatross 54
algae 2, 41
animals 8, 9
angelfish 13
anglerfish **16**, **48**
Arctic tern **55**
argonaut **33**
Atlantic Ocean 7
atoll **5**

barnacle **28**
barracuda **36**
bass **8**
benthos 9
bird **54**
bivalve 28
black swallower 19
blue whale **52**
breathing 12
bull shark **39**

chambered nautilus **29**
cleaner wrasse **14**, **18**
cod **37**
coelacanth **11**
conch shell **30**
continental shelf 34
cone snail **28**
copepod **9**
coral **40**
coral islands 5, 40
coral reef 40, 42, **44**
coral trout **14**
cowrie shell **30,** 31
crab 17, **26**
crocodile **58**
crown-of-thorns starfish 44
cuttlefish **32**

deep-sea fish **48**
diatom **9**
divers **4**, **6**, **43**
dogfish 13
dolphin **5**, **50**
dolphin fish **34**
dugong **59**

eel 13, **22**
eggs 35, 58
electric organs 38
elephant seal **61**
energy 7

fanworm **15**
fiddler crab **27**
fins 11

fish 10, 12, 14, 16, 20, 22, 38, 34, 38, 40, 48
fishing industry 7, 35, 37
flatfish **11**, **15**
flatworm **8**, 13
flounder **15**
flyingfish **18**
food, finding 16, 20, 28, 50, 54
fossils **8**, **11**
freshwater fish 14
fur seal **56**

gannet **54**
ghost crab **27**
giant kelp **8**, **24**, **25**
giant spider crab **60**
Great Barrier Reef **44**
great white shark **38**
grouper **36**, **43**
gull **54**

haddock **37**
halibut **37**
hermit crab **27**
herring **35**
humpback whale 52, **53**
hunters 16
hydromedusa **9**

iceberg **5**
iguana **58**
Indian Ocean 7
Irish moss **24**

jellyfish **12**, **61**
jet propulsion 33
jewfish **36**
John Dory **10**

kelp **8**, **24**, **25**
killer whale **50**, **51**

lamprey **10**
lanternfish **19**
lemon shark **12**
lionfish **17**
limpet **24**
lobster **24**, **26**

mammal 50, 54
manta ray **34**
marine fish 8, 14
marlin **35**
mermaid 59
migration 22, 55
minerals 7

mollusk 25, 30, 31
moray eel **10**, **42**
movement 13, 29
mussel **31**

narwhal **61**
nekton 9

oarfish **49**
ocean 4, 6, 24, 34, 48
ocean floor 6
octopus **9**, **32**
oil 7
osmosis 14
oyster **28**, 29

Pacific Ocean 7
parrotfish **43**
pearl **28**
penguin **55**
petrel **54**
plankton **9**, 16
plant 24
poisonous animals 16, 17, 29
polar seas 5
polyp 40
porcupine fish **19**
porpoise **51**
Portuguese man-of-war **20**
pufferfish **18**
puffin **54**

rain 7
ray 34, 38
reef **4**, 40, 42, 44
reef fish **41,42**
remora **12**
reptile **58**
right whale **52**

sailfish **60**
salmon 22, **23**
sardine **15**
sargassum fish **14**
sawfish **16**
scallop **31**
school **15**
scuba diving 43
sea anemone **21**
sea cucumber **21**
sea cow **59**
sea floor 24
sea lettuce **25**
sea lily **48**
sea lion **9**, **56**
sea otter **57**

sea pen **14**
sea serpent 49
sea snail 28, **29**
sea snake **59**
sea squirt **20**
sea turtle **9**,
sea urchin 25
sea wasp **61**
sea worm **8**
seahorse **20**
seal 56
seashore **4**, 24
seawater 4, 6
seaweed **8**, **24**, 25
shad **11**
shark 10, **12**,
shell 28, **29**, **30**, **31**
shrimp 26, **27**
skate 38
sole 11
sperm whale **53**
spider crab **8**
spiny lobster 24
sponge **46**
squid 33
starfish **8**, **24**, **25**
stargazer fish **16**
stingray **38**
stonefish **16**
sturgeon **22**
submersible **6**, 49
sunfish **37**
surfing **7**
swimming 13, 50
swordfish **34**

teeth 12, 38, 51
tentacles 20, 21, 32
Titanic (ship) 49
tooth shell **31**
triggerfish **43**
tripod fish **48**
tuna **13**
turtle **58**

univalve mollusk 28

vertebrate 10

walrus **57**
waves **4**, 7, 60
weeverfish **17**
whale **52**
whale shark **39**
whelk **30**
wolffish **36**
worm 8, 13
wrasse **14**, **18**

Picture acknowledgments
Cover: Peter Lake from Peter Schub; Mike Bacon, Tom Stack & Associates

Back Cover: WORLD BOOK photo (Academy of Natural Sciences of Philadelphia and Albert Lindar)

4 (top) © Barry E. Parker, Bruce Coleman; © Harvey Lloyd, The Stock Market. 5 (from top) © Alan Gurney, The Stock Market; © Karen Lukas, Photo Researchers; Lewis Wayne Walker. 6 Perry Oceanographics, Inc. 7 (top) © P. G. Ascogne, Agence Vandystadt from Photo Researchers; J. R. Eyerman, Black Star. 11 WORLD BOOK photo. 12 (top) Robert E. Pelham, Bruce Coleman; Marineland of Florida. 13 William M. Stevens, Tom Stack & Associates. 14 Margiocco from Paul Popper; Ben Cropp, Tom Stack & Associates. 15 Ron Church, Tom Stack & Associates; Runk/Schoenberger from Grant Heilman; G. Tomsich, Photo Researchers. 16 (top) © Doug Wechsler, Animals Animals; (bottom) Boyd Wells, Pictorial Parade; Giuseppe Mazza. 17 Stone/Deeble/Survival Anglia. 19 © David Hall, Photo Researchers. 20 (top) Maira and Rod Borland, Bruce Coleman; Kenneth H. R. Read, Tom Stack & Associates. 21 Al Goldings, Bruce Coleman; Jane Burton, Bruce Coleman. 23 © Johnny Johnson, DRK. 24 (top) Alex Kerstitch, Black Star; R. F. Thomas, Bruce Coleman. 25 (from top) Ben Cropp, Keystone; © Lewis Trusty, Animals Animals; Graham Lenton, Aquila. 26 (from top) George H. Harrison, Bruce Coleman; Oxford Scientific Films/Peter Parks; Oxford Scientific Films/Kathie Atkinson. 27 Des and Jean Bartlett, Bruce Coleman. 28 (top) Joy Spurr, Bruce Coleman; Sakata Pearl Co. (USA), Ltd. 29 (top) W. E. Townsend, Jr., Photo Researchers; P. Laboute, Jacana. 30-31 and cutaway on p.29 WORLD BOOK photos; specimens courtesy the Academy of Natural Sciences of Philadelphia and Albert Lindar. 32 © Fred Bavendon from Peter Arnold. 35 George H. Harrison from Grant Helman. 36 Jim Annan. 38 Larry Stessin, Photo Researchers. 39 Peter Lake from Peter Schub. 40 Douglas Faulkner. 40-41 Mike Bacon, Tom Stack & Associates. 42 Ben Cropp, Tom Stack & Associates. 43 © Carl Roessler. 44, 45 Photographic Library of Australia. 46 (from top) Mike Neumann, Photo Researchers; David Waselle, Journalism Services; Al Grotell; Al Grotell. 47 Al Grotell. 48 Carl Roessler, Animals Animals. 49 Woods Hole Oceanographic Institute. 51 Bruce Coleman; Wometco Miami Seaquarium. 52 Jean and Des Bartlett, Bruce Coleman. 53 James Hudnall. 54 Gordon Langsbury, Bruce Coleman; © Jeff Lepore, Photo Researchers. 55 William R. Curtsinger from Rapho Guillumette; Joyce Photographics from Photo Researchers. 56 Norman Tomalin, Bruce Coleman; Karl W. Kenyon, NAS. 57 R. H. Armstrong, Animals Animals. Steve McCutcheon. 58 William M. Stephen, Tom Stack & Associates; Mel Zaloudek from Marilyn Gartman. 59 Bill Wood, Bruce Coleman. 60 Tom Stack. 61 Cy La Tour; Bob and Valerie Taylor, Bruce Coleman.

Illustrations
By WORLD BOOK artists including John Dawson, John F. Eggert, Alan Male, Harry McNaught, Donald Moss, Colin Newman, Marion Pahl, John Rignall, James Teason, and Sarah Woodward.